LEGO STAR WARS

THE YODA CHRONICLES

Written by DANIEL LIPKOWITZ

CONTENTS

INTRODUCTION

Teacher. General. Grand Master.

One of the wisest and most mysterious beings in the galaxy, Yoda has accomplished many things over the course of his 900 years. He has led the Jedi High Council. He has commanded armies into battle. He has trained thousands of aspiring Jedi Knights. He has hidden in obscurity on a forgotten swamp planet. He has made great friends and dangerous foes—and met others, like the curious Jek-14, whose allegiance lay somewhere in between.

From the golden days of the Galactic Republic, through the chaos of the Clone Wars and the evil rule of the Empire, Yoda's influence on galactic events is as important and far-reaching as the little Jedi Master himself.

This is Yoda's story.

NOTE ON DATES
Dates are fixed around the Battle of Yavin in year 0. The dates recorded in this book are measured in terms of years Before the Battle of Yavin (BBY), when the first Death Star was destroyed by Luke Skywalker and the Rebel Alliance.

PATH OF KNOWLEDGE

Most Jedi receive training from Yoda as younglings but only a few are chosen as his official Padawan apprentices. As his students have become Masters and taught apprentices of their own, Yoda's teachings have been passed down through generations of Jedi.

WHO TAUGHT WHO?

YODA

COUNT DOOKU

LUKE SKYWALKER

KI-ADI-MUNDI

CAN I BE EXCUSED, MASTER YODA? MY HEAD IS FULL.

QUI-GON JINN

OBI-WAN KENOBI

ANAKIN SKYWALKER

SO IN A WAY, YODA TRAINED ME TOO!

AHSOKA TANO

HOBBIES

Yoda's life isn't all hard work and fighting. He also enjoys cooking and reading the latest Jedi periodicals.

YODA

YODA IS ONE of the greatest Jedi Masters ever known. His power with the Force and talent with a lightsaber are matched only by his vast wisdom and compassion. The Grand Master is always willing to teach those who have the patience to listen.

IN BATTLE

Many enemies underestimate Yoda because of his size and age. Little do they know that when he finally cuts loose, he becomes a leaping, bouncing, lightsaber-swinging blur of Jedi fighting skill!

"A JEDI MUST HAVE THE DEEPEST COMMITMENT, THE MOST SERIOUS MIND."

YODA

Natural crystals create green blade

DATA FILE

HOMEWORLD: UNKNOWN

BIRTH DATE: 896 BBY

RANK: GRAND MASTER

TRAINED BY: UNKNOWN

WEAPON: GREEN-BLADED LIGHTSABER

Tan outer robes and brown undershirt

PORTRAIT OF A JEDI
Yoda has a reptilian appearance, a wrinkled and bumpy forehead, long, pointed ears, and wispy gray hair on the back of his head. Like most Jedi, Yoda dresses in simple, durable robes.

TOOL OF THE TRADE
900-year-old Yoda walks with the aid of a wooden gimer stick. Not only can it double as a weapon, but Yoda also chews on it for a nutritious snack.

Yoda can use the Force to draw his **lightsaber** from his robes into his hand. He is a **master** of the **Ataru** lightsaber form, which involves **Force leaps**, twirls, and twists.

SNEAK UP ON ME YOU CANNOT. SENSE YOU I CAN!

7

WHERE DOES YODA COME FROM?

Yoda is not the only member of his species to become a Jedi. Others are known, including the female Yaddle, who also served on the Jedi Council.

IT'S A QUESTION that many of his friends and enemies have asked. All that is known of Yoda's homeworld is that its inhabitants are green-skinned and short in stature, with very long lifespans and a high sensitivity to the Force. So where does he really come from? Everybody has a different theory!

?

TELLING I AM NOT!

I JUST THOUGHT YODA CAME FROM THE SWAMPS OF DAGOBAH WHERE I MET HIM. WHO KNEW HE HAD BEEN ON ADVENTURES ALL OVER THE GALAXY BEFORE THAT?

LUKE SKYWALKER

I FIGURE HE COMES FROM THE PLANET OF CRANKY LITTLE GREEN GUYS, WHERE EVERYBODY TALKS FUNNY AND HAS A STRANGE SENSE OF HUMOR.

YOUNG HAN SOLO

CHANCELLOR PALPATINE

WHEREVER HE COMES FROM, I HOPE THERE AREN'T ANY MORE OF HIM OUT THERE.

MACE WINDU

THE OTHER COUNCIL MEMBERS AND I ARE ALWAYS TRYING TO GET HIM TO TELL US WHERE HE COMES FROM, BUT HE WON'T SAY. I THINK HE LIKES ALL THE ATTENTION.

QUI-GON JINN

CLONE TROOPER

YODA NEVER SAID ANYTHING ABOUT HIS HOME PLANET DURING MY TRAINING. IT MADE ME WONDER IF IT HAD BEEN DESTROYED A LONG TIME AGO ...

HE'S A LITTLE GREEN LIZARD GUY, SO MAYBE HE'S FROM TATOOINE WHERE THOSE DEWBACKS COME FROM. THEY'RE GREEN LIZARDS TOO, RIGHT?

C-3PO

I AM FLUENT IN MORE THAN SIX MILLION FORMS OF COMMUNICATION, BUT AS FAR AS I AM CONCERNED, MASTER YODA IS ENTIRELY UNIQUE IN THE GALAXY!

CHEWBACCA

AOOOGH ROOAAAR GRAAGH RUH.*

* TRANSLATION: I KNOW WHERE HE'S FROM, BUT I'M NOT TELLING.

MACE WINDU

LEGENDARY JEDI MASTER Mace Windu is respected throughout the galaxy for his wisdom, courage, and skill with a lightsaber. Mace was the head of the Jedi Council before Yoda but he stepped down to lead troops in the Clone Wars.

A TRUSTED FRIEND

Mace is Yoda's second-in-command. When Yoda goes on an emergency rescue mission to Alderaan, Mace is the first Jedi he calls on for help. Mace and Yoda often trade wisdom and advice. They both sense Anakin Skywalker's strong emotional attachments and fear for the young Jedi's future.

Rare purple lightsaber blade

Jedi tunic

> **"THE** OPPRESSION OF THE SITH WILL **NEVER** RETURN!**"**
>
> MACE WINDU TO DARTH SIDIOUS

DATA FILE

- **HOMEWORLD:** HARUUN KAL
- **BIRTH DATE:** 72 BBY
- **RANK:** JEDI MASTER
- **TRAINED BY:** UNKNOWN
- **WEAPON:** PURPLE-BLADED LIGHTSABER

PALPATINE'S ARREST

Yoda respects Mace's loyalty and commitment to justice and the Jedi Order. When Mace learns that Supreme Chancellor Palpatine is a Sith Lord, he tries to arrest him. Unfortunately for Mace, his doubts about Anakin Skywalker prove to be correct. The young Jedi interferes in his duel against Palpatine and sides with the Sith.

Kit Fisto

Saesee Tiin

Agen Kolar

I WILL DISASSEMBLE THE REPUBLIC!

Chancellor Palpatine

NOT IF I DISASSEMBLE YOU FIRST!

Holoprojector

Bronzium statue

Mace Windu

Like **Yoda**, Mace prefers to resolve conflict through **negotiation**. But when the Jedi are forced into **war**, Mace doesn't hesitate to **fight** for the things he **believes** in.

I KNEW I'D COME OUT "AHEAD" IN THIS DUEL.

IT'S A GOOD THING THIS POPS BACK ON!

BATTLE OF GEONOSIS

As the Clone Wars begin, Yoda and Mace come up with a two-part plan to stop the Separatist Droid Army on Geonosis. While Yoda goes to gather an army of clone troopers, Mace leads a strike force of Jedi Knights in a direct attack. During the battle, the master duelist faces and defeats infamous bounty hunter Jango Fett.

11

SMALL BUT MIGHTY

YODA MAY NOT be very tall, but what he lacks in height, he more than makes up for in power. His ability to channel the Force enables this aged Jedi Grand Master to leap great distances, perform acrobatic stunts, deflect weapon fire, and defeat his enemies in battle.

> **"SIZE MATTERS NOT.** LOOK AT ME. JUDGE ME BY MY SIZE, DO YOU?"
>
> YODA

| Yoda | Gamorrean Guard | Rancor |

SMALL SIZE, BIG POWER
It's easy to underestimate Yoda. In most of the galaxy, the bigger something is, the tougher it is. But when it comes to a Jedi, what matters most is their ability to sense and channel the Force.

UP YOUR SLEEVES, ANY MORE TRICKS DO YOU HAVE?

Sith lightning

Floating Senate pod

FORCE PUSH

Thanks to his ability to push and pull objects using the Force, Yoda does not even need to lay his hands on his enemies to make them move out of his way. When Emperor Palpatine's guards try to stop him in the Senate building, Yoda has only to gesture —and they go flying!

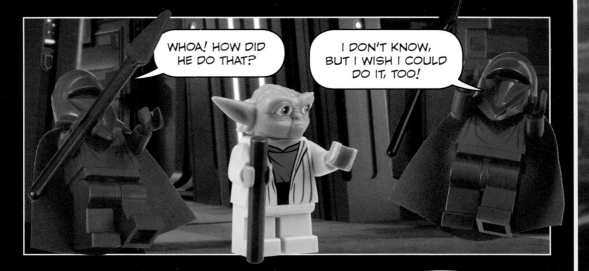

WHOA! HOW DID HE DO THAT?

I DON'T KNOW, BUT I WISH I COULD DO IT, TOO!

Darth Sidious

HUH?! I CAN'T UNDERSTAND WHAT YOU'RE SAYING!

FORCE BUILDING

The Force binds everything in the galaxy together, but it can be used to take things apart as well. A highly Force-sensitive Jedi such as Yoda can use his powers to disassemble objects and rebuild them in different ways to make walls, cages, stairs, and even spaceships.

The Force is an invisible **energy** field that flows through every living being. Jedi are very **sensitive** to the **Force**. They spend years in deep **study** learning how to harness it in different ways.

FORCE DEFLECTION

Even without his lightsaber, Yoda is far from defenseless. He can use the Force to redirect all kinds of attacks—from blaster bolts and projectiles to the Force lightning wielded by Dark Lords of the Sith. When Darth Sidious hurls the deadly power of the dark side at him, Yoda simply catches it in his hands and gathers it up to throw back at him!

OBI-WAN KENOBI

Being a **Jedi** isn't all fighting and **starfighter duels**. Between missions, Obi-Wan likes to kick back and **relax** by the poolside on **Alderaan**.

Double-bladed Sith lightsaber

MUCH LIKE YODA, Obi-Wan Kenobi embodies the values of the Jedi Knights. He is calm, humble, and loyal to the Jedi Order. Despite this dedication, he never loses his sense of humor and doesn't hesitate to take risks to protect his friends.

BATTLE WITH DARTH MAUL
As a Padawan, Obi-Wan has to face the merciless dark side warrior Darth Maul. Obi-Wan's courage and skill in overcoming such a powerful opponent lead Yoda and the Jedi Council to make him a full Jedi Knight. Although Yoda has reservations about Anakin Skywalker, the Council also agrees to let Anakin become Obi-Wan's apprentice.

A BAD FEELING ...

Obi-Wan's talent with words and reason and his ability to sense the feelings of others make him a clever negotiator. Unfortunately, negotiations are useless against hostile droids—so sometimes even the most peaceful Jedi must take up his lightsaber to do battle. Luckily, this is something else at which Obi-Wan excels!

QUI-GON JINN

Obi-Wan's wise Master is attuned to the living Force and lets his instincts guide his actions. Yoda does not always agree with Qui-Gon's decisions, but he respects him greatly.

> SO MY FATHER WAS A GREAT JEDI HERO?

> ER ... AMONG OTHER THINGS, LUKE ...

Luke's X-34 landspeeder

IN EXILE

After the fall of the Republic and the destruction of most of the Jedi, Obi-Wan goes into hiding. He lives as desert hermit Ben Kenobi on Tatooine. But the old Jedi Master secretly watches over Luke Skywalker, preparing for the day when Luke will be ready to be trained by Yoda as a Jedi.

Utility belt

Simple Jedi robe

LIFETIME OF SERVICE

Obi-Wan earns a galaxy-wide reputation as one of the greatest Jedi of all time. After his impressive feats as a Padawan, Obi-Wan leads troops to many victories in the Clone Wars, and becomes an important member of the Jedi Council.

DATA FILE

- **HOMEWORLD:** STEWJON
- **BIRTH DATE:** 57 BBY
- **RANK:** JEDI MASTER
- **TRAINED BY:** QUI-GON JINN
- **WEAPON:** BLUE-BLADED LIGHTSABER

YODA'S WISDOM

YODA ISN'T THE BIGGEST Jedi Master around, but he is definitely one of the wisest. Although his way of speaking can sometimes be a little hard to follow, a Padawan who pays close attention to Yoda's teachings will become a great Jedi Knight.

> "FEAR IS THE PATH TO THE DARK SIDE. FEAR LEADS TO ANGER. ANGER LEADS TO HATE. HATE LEADS TO SUFFERING."

> "Do. Or do not. There is no try."

> "WARS NOT MAKE ONE GREAT."

"My ally is the Force, and a powerful ally it is."

"ADVENTURE. EXCITEMENT. A JEDI CRAVES NOT THESE THINGS."

"When 900 years old you reach, look as good you will not."

"A JEDI USES THE FORCE FOR KNOWLEDGE AND DEFENSE, NEVER FOR ATTACK."

"Smaller in number we are, but larger in mind."

"EVERYTHING YOU FEAR TO LOSE, LEARN TO LET GO OF YOU MUST."

"To answer power with power, the Jedi way this is not."

"IF ONCE YOU START DOWN THE DARK PATH, FOREVER WILL IT DOMINATE YOUR DESTINY."

DATA FILE

- **HOMEWORLD:** TATOOINE
- **BIRTH DATE:** 41 BBY
- **RANK:** JEDI KNIGHT
- **TRAINED BY:** OBI-WAN KENOBI
- **WEAPON:** BLUE BLADED LIGHTSABER

CLOUDED, HIS FUTURE IS

Yoda is concerned about Anakin's destiny because he has trouble controlling his anger and takes too many risks. The young Jedi attacks a whole camp of Tusken Raiders after he discovers they caused his mother's death.

Battle-scarred face

HERO WITH NO FEAR

Anakin is a hero to the Padawans in Yoda's classroom. They love watching Holocron recordings of his adventures. Anakin may be courageous, but his recklessness and overconfidence can get him into trouble, especially against skilled opponents such as Count Dooku or the Force-enhanced clone Jek-14.

YODA'S ALLIES

ANAKIN SKYWALKER

AS A YOUNG SLAVE BOY on Tatooine, Anakin learns that he is the "Chosen One" who will bring balance to the Force. Anakin grows up to be one of the greatest Jedi ever known, but Yoda worries about his future …

DON'T WORRY, OBI-WAN. I'LL SAVE YOU!

Obi-Wan and Anakin must battle through an armada of Separatist droid fighters to save Palpatine.

YOU'RE CUTTING IT CLOSE, ANAKIN ...BUT NOT AS CLOSE AS THIS BUZZ DROID!

Like all battle droids, Vulture droids attack in large numbers.

FAITHFUL APPRENTICE

During the Clone Wars, Yoda assigns Anakin a Padawan in an effort to teach him about control and responsibility. Feisty Ahsoka Tano—nicknamed "Snips" by Anakin—is a quick learner and shows great promise, but she is headstrong like her master.

JEDI GENERAL

Despite his concerns about Anakin, Yoda must admit that he is a great fighter and general. Anakin is an expert pilot from a young age and flies to victory in many Clone Wars missions. During the Battle of Coruscant, Anakin and his Master, Obi-Wan Kenobi, survive a threat from a swarm of enemy ships to rescue Chancellor Palpatine from General Grievous.

BECOMING VADER

Yoda's worst fears eventually come true when Anakin falls to the dark side. Badly injured after dueling Obi-Wan, Anakin is rebuilt as the powerful Sith Lord Darth Vader, a deadly enemy to Jedi everywhere.

YODA THE TEACHER

IN HIS EIGHT CENTURIES of teaching, Yoda has instructed many Padawans, including some of the most famous Jedi of all time. Yoda is a natural teacher and is dedicated to providing generations of Padawans with the knowledge, skills, and attitude to become Jedi.

Holocrons project stories and information

Mechanical podium raises and lowers

HISTORY LESSON

The students in Yoda's classes do not always understand the meanings of his lectures at first. But as they grow older and wiser, they will come to appreciate their earliest lessons. One of the students' favorite classrooms is the Holocron Vault in the Jedi Temple, where they can watch holographic recordings from the long history of the Jedi Order.

YODA'S PADAWANS
New Jedi initiates are placed in clans that attend classes and training together. One of these is the Bear Clan, a group of brave younglings from different worlds. These young students have already had more adventures than many Jedi Knights twice their age.

WHAT MAKES A GOOD STUDENT?

Yoda requires more from his students than just great skill. Although young Anakin Skywalker is an excellent pilot with a very powerful connection to the Force, Yoda feels that his lateness to Jedi training and his overpowering emotions make him a poor candidate to become a Jedi.

THE ULTIMATE TEST

Yoda knows that no matter how well a student does at the Academy, the real test can be found only outside the safety of the Jedi Temple. When Anakin becomes the apprentice of Obi-Wan Kenobi, he risks his life chasing the shape-shifting bounty hunter Zam Wesell on Coruscant.

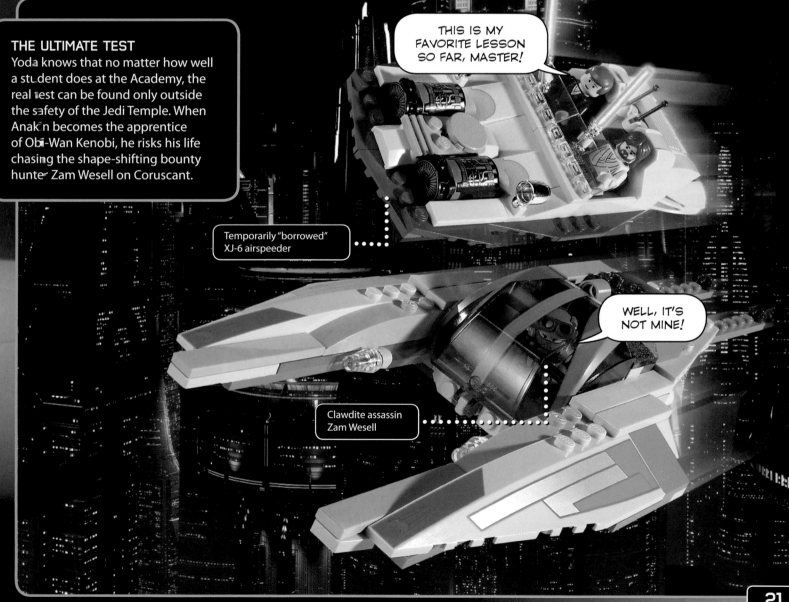

THIS IS MY FAVORITE LESSON SO FAR, MASTER!

WELL, IT'S NOT MINE!

Temporarily "borrowed" XJ-6 airspeeder

Clawdite assassin Zam Wesell

COULD YOU BE ONE OF YODA'S PADAWANS?

WOULD YOU MAKE a good Padawan? Not every student can pass Yoda's class and become a true Jedi. Answer Yoda's questions and discover your own path through Jedi training!

READY TO LEARN THE WAYS OF THE FORCE, YOU ARE?

YES

MUCH HOMEWORK THERE WILL BE. FEAR THIS DO YOU?

NO

YES

BUT TRAIN WOULD YOU, TO PROTECT THE GALAXY?

YES

AMAZING ARE JEDI POWERS. LOOK FORWARD TO PLAYING WITH THEM, DO YOU?

NO

FUNNY DO YOU FIND MASTER WINDU'S BALD HEAD? HMMM?

NO →

YES

NO

NO

JEDI MASTER
The seeds of greatness in you, I see. Perhaps one day, beside me on the Jedi Council sit you will.

JEDI KNIGHT
Already well on your way to becoming a Jedi are you, but train must you still. A brave warrior will you be.

BETTER IT IS TO BE BIG THAN SMALL. AGREE WITH THIS DO YOU?

YES

INITIATE
Much to learn, you have. Fortunately, much to teach I have. At the beginner level of my class start will you.

NO

"BADAWAN"
A touch of the dark side I sense. Think inwardly you must, and decide why wish to be a Jedi you do.

YES

TEACH YOU, I CANNOT
Sadly, the makings of a Jedi you lack. Perhaps better suited to the Agricultural Corps, you would be?

23

CHANCELLOR PALPATINE

YODA AND THE OTHER Jedi know Palpatine as the kindly Supreme Chancellor of the Galactic Republic. But Palpatine is secretly Darth Sidious—a Dark Lord of the Sith who steers events from behind the scenes to achieve his goal of controlling the galaxy.

Formal Chancellor's garb

Stabilizer fin

Electrum-plated handle

Wings fold up for landing

Laser cannons

PALPATINE'S SHUTTLE
Officially, Palpatine's *Theta*-class T-2c shuttle carries him on Senate business. But it's also handy for sneaky escapes when his identity as Darth Sidious is about to be exposed.

DARK DECEIVER
Few can deceive a 900-year-old Jedi Master, but Palpatine is so strong in the dark side of the Force that not even Yoda suspects his true evil nature. He uses his cover to manipulate the Jedi, for example by giving them false information or sending them into Separatist traps.

AREN'T YOU A LITTLE SMALL FOR A JEDI MASTER?

AS SHORT AS ME, YOUR REIGN WILL BE!

RISE OF THE EMPEROR

When the pieces of his plan have come together, Palpatine betrays the Jedi and installs himself as Emperor of a new Galactic Empire. Seeing one last chance to confront the Sith Lord and restore peace to the galaxy, Yoda duels with him in the Senate building on Coruscant—but he is outmatched by the Emperor's rage and power.

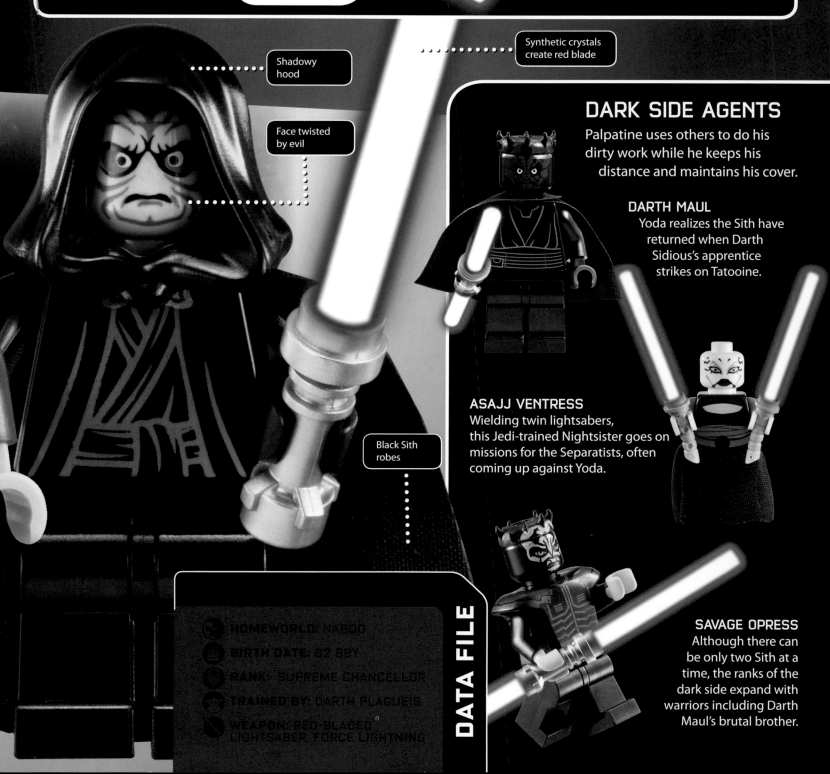

Shadowy hood

Synthetic crystals create red blade

Face twisted by evil

Black Sith robes

DARK SIDE AGENTS

Palpatine uses others to do his dirty work while he keeps his distance and maintains his cover.

DARTH MAUL

Yoda realizes the Sith have returned when Darth Sidious's apprentice strikes on Tatooine.

ASAJJ VENTRESS

Wielding twin lightsabers, this Jedi-trained Nightsister goes on missions for the Separatists, often coming up against Yoda.

SAVAGE OPRESS

Although there can be only two Sith at a time, the ranks of the dark side expand with warriors including Darth Maul's brutal brother.

DATA FILE

- HOMEWORLD: NABOO
- BIRTH DATE: 82 BBY
- RANK: SUPREME CHANCELLOR
- TRAINED BY: DARTH PLAGUEIS
- WEAPON: RED-BLADED LIGHTSABER, FORCE LIGHTNING

HOMEWORLD: SERENNO

BIRTH DATE: 102 BBY

RANK: SITH LORD, FORMER JEDI MASTER

TRAINED BY: YODA FOLLOWED BY DARTH SIDIOUS

WEAPON: RED-BLADED LIGHTSABER

COUNT DOOKU

TO YODA AND MOST of the galaxy, Count Dooku is the head of the Separatists, a nobleman and former Jedi who leads the attack against the Republic. But like his master Palpatine, Dooku leads a double life—as the Sith apprentice Darth Tyranus.

JEDI TURNCOAT

When Dooku was a Jedi Padawan, he learned the art of lightsaber combat from Yoda himself. That is how he knows of the Kyber crystals hidden in the lightsabers of Yoda's pupils—and how Yoda realizes that his former student is responsible when they are stolen by General Grievous.

Royal tunic lined with armorweave

Curved-hilt lightsaber

SOLAR SAILER
Dooku's Geonosian *Punworcca 116*-class interstellar sloop has a solar sail that propels it silently through space.

STUDENT VS. MASTER

When Yoda and Dooku confront each other during the first battle of the Clone Wars, the Count has grown strong in the dark side of the Force. But as the teacher and his former Padawan duel with Force powers and lightsaber blades, it quickly becomes clear that Yoda is still the master.

> WHEN LAST WE MET, I WAS BUT THE LEARNER ...

> THE WRONG MOVIE, THAT IS!

Having **lost** Dooku to the **dark side**, Yoda works hard to make sure his younglings understand the difference between **right** and **wrong**.

PLAN FOR DOMINATION

Dooku's talent with a lightsaber is rivaled only by his intelligence and cunning. His knowledge of technology aids him in his scheme for the stolen Kyber crystals. He plans to use them to build an army of loyal Force-enhanced clone warriors to fight alongside the Sith—starting with Jek-14!

A SPEEDY GETAWAY

Like any good villain, Dooku knows when to stand and fight, and when it's better to turn tail and run. If the odds are against him, he hops on his modified Flitknot speeder and flees to safety.

Geonosian design

Stabilizer fins

YODA THE GRAND MASTER

> LONG HOURS, THIS JOB HAS ... BUT LOOKING FORWARD TO RETIRING ON A SWAMP PLANET, I AM NOT!

LEGENDARY LEADER

To become Grand Master, a Jedi must receive a unanimous vote from the entire Jedi Council and display the highest degree of wisdom, skill, and responsibility. During the Clone Wars, Yoda has to lead his fellow Jedi in both peace and battle.

SAESEE TIIN

A horned, telepathic Iktotchi, Saesee Tiin is an important member of the Jedi Council. He is a brave soldier and celebrated starfighter pilot. Tiin's mind-reading abilities give him a natural advantage in both space and lightsaber combat.

KI-ADI-MUNDI

As a Cerean, Ki-Adi-Mundi has a binary brain in his large head that helps him to focus on multiple tasks at the same time. Unlike most Jedi, he joined the Council as a Knight before reaching the rank of Master.

KIT FISTO

Kit Fisto is an amphibious Nautolan who is equally at home in water and on land. His victories as a general in the Clone Wars lead to his appointment to the Jedi High Council—although he is too modest to accept at first!

SHAAK TI

Shaak Ti is a Togruta member of the Jedi Council. She often takes on missions of defense, whether rescuing captured allies, protecting new clone troopers on Kamino, or safeguarding the Jedi Temple from attack.

AGEN KOLAR

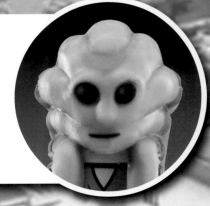

Like fellow Council member Eeth Koth, Agen Kolar is a Zabrak. Kolar prefers fighting to discussion and negotiation and is often the first to ignite his lightsaber. He is almost as good a duelist as the legendary Mace Windu.

YODA IS THE GRAND MASTER

of the Jedi Order, a position that holds great honor and respect. Yoda works alongside the wisest and most skilled Jedi on the Council. Together, they select other talented Jedi to undertake special missions, plan military strategies in times of war, and seek guidance from the Force.

THE JEDI COUNCIL
The Jedi High Council is made up of 12 exemplary Jedi Masters who are elected to guide the Jedi Order. The Council members meet in the Jedi Temple on Coruscant to discuss matters of importance to the Republic and to advise the Supreme Chancellor, the leader of the Republic.

EETH KOTH
When he was first brought before the High Council as a child, Eeth Koth was thought to be too old for Jedi training. Fortunately, the strong Force-user proved his worth and he has even gone on to serve on the Council himself.

EVEN PIELL
Jedi Council member Even Piell shows a fearlessness in battle that more than makes up for his small stature. The battle-worn Jedi's long Lannik ears give him super-sensitive hearing.

PLO KOON
A Jedi Council member of the Kel Dor species, Plo Koon has to wear a special mask to see and breathe when off his home planet. Koon has a strong sense of justice and is skilled at moving objects using the Force.

AAYLA SECURA
A Twi'lek Jedi Master, Aayla Secura has confronted and overcome the temptations of the dark side of the Force. She is intelligent and a talented lightsaber wielder, but she still retains a mischievous streak.

LUMINARA UNDULI
Mirialan Jedi Master Luminara Unduli leads her clone troopers alongside Yoda during the Battle of Kashyyyk. Her chin tattoos symbolize her dedication to constantly improving her physical skills.

BARISS OFFEE
As Master Unduli's Padawan apprentice, Bariss Offee has already seen much of the chaos caused by warfare. That is why she has trained to be a Jedi healer. Her Mirialan facial tattoos signify her achievements as a healer.

Holoprojector

Starship linkage arms

Barrel-like body filled with hidden tools and gadgets

Recharge coupling

SECRET WEDDING
When Anakin Skywalker and Padmé Amidala ignore the Jedi Codeand get married, they exchange droids. R2-D2 becomes Anakin's assistant, and C-3PO Padmé's. The two droids keep the secret so well that even Yoda doesn't know about the wedding!

DATA FILE

HOMEWORLD: NABOO

CREATION DATE: AROUND 33 BBY

DROID TYPE: R2-SERIES ASTROMECH DROID

BUILT BY: INDUSTRIAL AUTOMATON

EQUIPMENT: BUZZ SAW, FUSION WELDER, THRUSTER JETS, AND MORE

R2-D2
This brave beeping and buzzing little droid is always ready to help his friends, and often notices what others miss. He may even suspect the truth about Chancellor Palpatine … but if so, he hasn't had any luck telling anyone!

R2-D2 AND C-3PO

YODA HAS MET a lot of droids in his long lifetime, but none quite like this unusual pair. "Artoo" and "Threepio" have had adventures across the galaxy, somehow ending up right in the middle of the action no matter where they go.

CO-PILOT
As an astromech droid, R2-D2 is programmed to repair and navigate starships. His gadgets, inventiveness, and heroism often save the day in the heat of battle.

Class-6 escape pod

OH, NO. I'M NOT GOING ANYWHERE UNTIL YOU PUT THIS POD BACK TOGETHER AND FLY US OUT OF HERE!

WHEE-OO BLEEP!

ESCAPE TO TATOOINE

While Yoda is dwelling as a hermit on Dagobah, R2-D2 and C-3PO get caught up in yet another battle for the fate of the galaxy. Artoo becomes a key agent of the Rebel Alliance and the guardian of the plans to the Empire's ultimate weapon: the Death Star! He leads C-3PO on a journey through the desert of Tatooine to deliver the plans to Obi-Wan Kenobi.

Photoreceptor

Vocabulator

Exposed connection wires

C-3PO

A protocol droid who knows more than 6 million forms of communication, C-3PO is proper, polite, and constantly worried. He never asked for excitement, but it keeps finding him. All things considered, he'd much rather relax in a nice hot oil bath!

SUBSTITUTE TEACHER

Since he was first assembled by Anakin, poor C-3PO has seemed to face one peril after another. Still, he's rarely encountered as dangerous a mission as having to substitute-teach Yoda's class of unruly Jedi trainees ... not to mention drive their school bus!

DATA FILE

HOMEWORLD: TATOOINE

CREATION DATE: 112 BBY, REBUILT 32 BBY

DROID TYPE: 3PO-SERIES PROTOCOL DROID

BUILT BY: CYBOT GALACTICA (REBUILT BY ANAKIN SKYWALKER)

EQUIPMENT: NONE

GENERAL GRIEVOUS

YODA HAS RARELY faced an enemy as filled with hate as the savage cyborg Grievous. The terrifying Supreme Commander of the Separatist Droid Army delights in causing mayhem and trouble —especially for the Jedi.

Eyes from original body

Stolen Jedi lightsaber

Mask-like face plate

A MATCH FOR THE JEDI

Grievous was once an organic being, but he chose to be rebuilt as a cyborg after he almost died in a shuttle crash. He had always been jealous of the Jedi's abilities, and now his cyborg body would be strong enough to fight them. Even so, Grievous knows how powerful Yoda is, and prefers to avoid directly challenging the skilled Jedi Master.

Duranium alloy body

Clawed feet

DATA FILE

What does a **wise** Jedi Master do when faced with an opponent with four whirling **lightsabers**? **Easy**—Yoda uses his lightsaber to **slice** the floor out from under his foe!

LIGHTSABERS

Grievous may not be Force-sensitive, but he is deadly with a lightsaber. His prized possession is his collection of Jedi lightsabers, each taken from a defeated foe. He's evil enough to even steal the lightsabers of Jedi Padawans.

Command bridge

Ion pulse cannon

THE *MALEVOLENCE*

A secret Separatist super-weapon, the *Malevolence* is one of General Grievous's flagships. It is armed with a pair of giant ion pulse cannons that can knock out the power of an entire Republic fleet.

The super-weapon is longer than four Republic *Venator*-class Star Destroyers.

Ion drive

Single-pilot cockpit

GRIEVOUS'S STARFIGHTER

When a task calls for his own personal touch, General Grievous makes use of his modified Belbullab-22 starfighter, the *Soulless One*. Its enhanced hyperdrive transports him swiftly across the galaxy as he carries out the sinister plans of Count Dooku and Darth Sidious.

Laser cannon

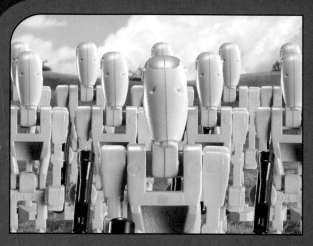

DROID ARMY

Grievous may resemble a droid, but that doesn't mean he has to like them. His favorite hobby is shouting at his battle droids and ordering them into battle. And if Yoda and the other Jedi destroy the droids, then who cares? The Separatists can always make more.

THE GALAXY IS FULL of heroes and villains. Somewhere in the middle are the unscrupulous rogues and mercenaries whose loyalties lie with whichever side pays them the most. Many choose to fight for Yoda's enemies, but even the Jedi can use a little extra help sometimes.

Turk Falso

SPACE PIRATES
Hondo Ohnaka and his pirate band may be troublemaking crooks, but they have their own odd sense of honor and can be handy allies … for the right price.

WLO-5 pirate tank

Heavy laser turret

Hondo Ohnaka

WHO INVITED SHAHAN INTO THIS LINEUP?

BEST BOUNTY HUNTERS IN THE BUSINESS

CAD BANE
One of the most feared bounty hunters. Cross him at your peril!

EMBO
An athletic fighter whose hat serves as a shield and a throwing weapon.

AURRA SING
A former Jedi Padawan turned bounty hunter and assassin.

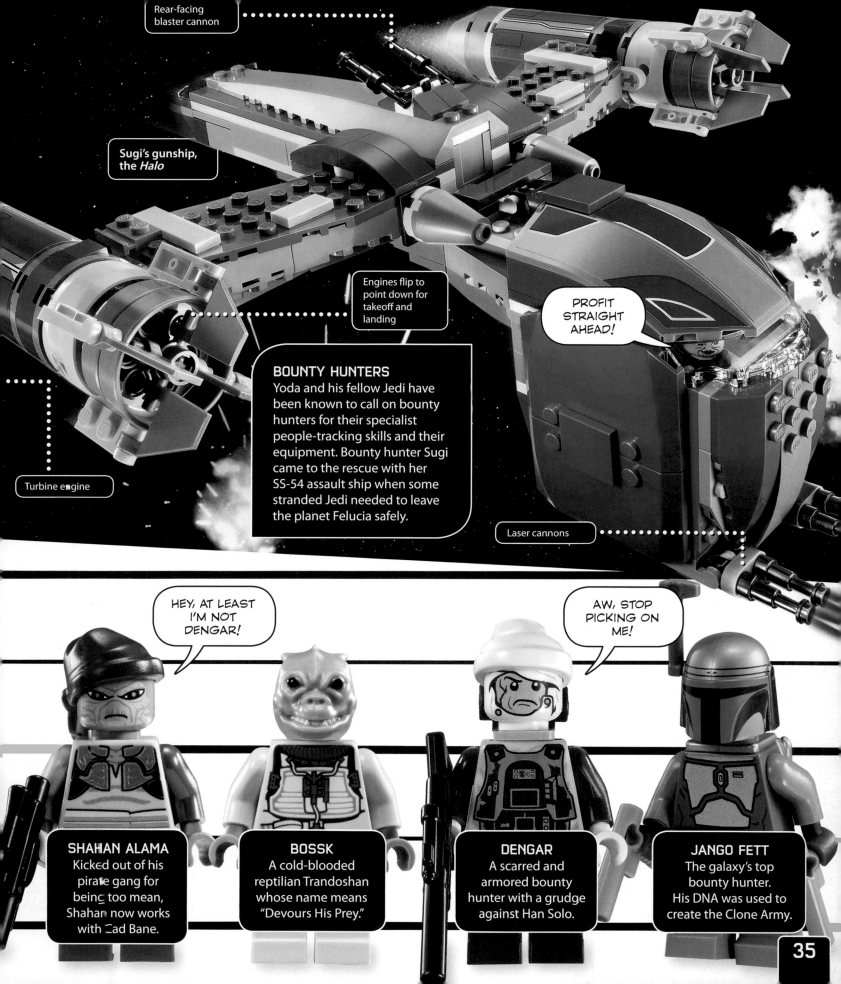

Rear-facing blaster cannon

Sugi's gunship, the *Halo*

Engines flip to point down for takeoff and landing

Turbine engine

PROFIT STRAIGHT AHEAD!

BOUNTY HUNTERS
Yoda and his fellow Jedi have been known to call on bounty hunters for their specialist people-tracking skills and their equipment. Bounty hunter Sugi came to the rescue with her SS-54 assault ship when some stranded Jedi needed to leave the planet Felucia safely.

Laser cannons

HEY, AT LEAST I'M NOT DENGAR!

AW, STOP PICKING ON ME!

SHAHAN ALAMA
Kicked out of his pirate gang for being too mean, Shahan now works with Cad Bane.

BOSSK
A cold-blooded reptilian Trandoshan whose name means "Devours His Prey."

DENGAR
A scarred and armored bounty hunter with a grudge against Han Solo.

JANGO FETT
The galaxy's top bounty hunter. His DNA was used to create the Clone Army.

YODA THE GENERAL

YODA DOES NOT like to use violence, but he will fight to defend the Republic and the Jedi Order. When the Clone Wars begin, he becomes the reluctant leader of Jedi generals and an army of clone troopers.

Firing proton torpedo

HERE'S THE SHUTTLE. WHO CALLED FOR A LIFT?

Mace Windu

ALL CLONES— ATTACK!

Clone trooper

Nu-class Republic attack shuttle

Commander Gree

WE GET SWEET EXTRA GEAR, TOO!

Commander Cod

OFFICER CLASS

Many Jedi serve as generals of the Clone Army. The clone officers who report to the Jedi often distinguish themselves enough to receive their own unique nicknames and armor markings. Commander Cody of the 212th Attack Battalion sometimes accompanies Yoda on his missions.

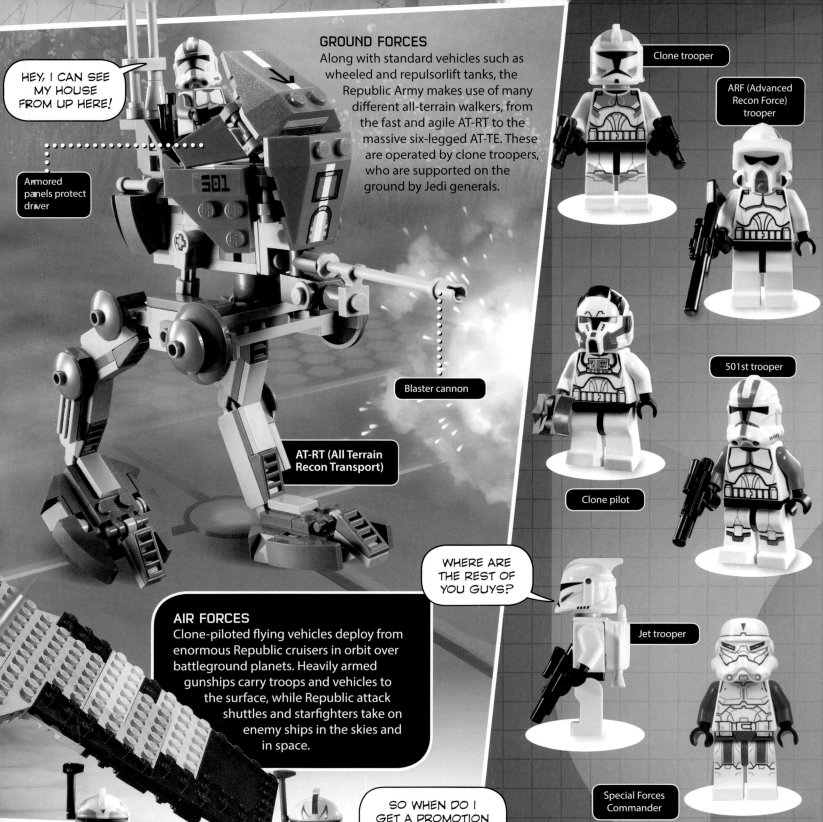

GROUND FORCES
Along with standard vehicles such as wheeled and repulsorlift tanks, the Republic Army makes use of many different all-terrain walkers, from the fast and agile AT-RT to the massive six-legged AT-TE. These are operated by clone troopers, who are supported on the ground by Jedi generals.

HEY, I CAN SEE MY HOUSE FROM UP HERE!

Armored panels protect driver

Blaster cannon

AT-RT (All Terrain Recon Transport)

Clone trooper

ARF (Advanced Recon Force) trooper

501st trooper

Clone pilot

Jet trooper

Special Forces Commander

WHERE ARE THE REST OF YOU GUYS?

AIR FORCES
Clone-piloted flying vehicles deploy from enormous Republic cruisers in orbit over battleground planets. Heavily armed gunships carry troops and vehicles to the surface, while Republic attack shuttles and starfighters take on enemy ships in the skies and in space.

Commander Wolffe

SO WHEN DO I GET A PROMOTION TO COMMANDER?

Captain Rex

SPECIALIST CLONES
They may have identical faces under their helmets, but not every clone trooper is the same. Some receive training and equipment for special jobs, such as piloting vehicles, scouting hostile environments, and handling heavy weaponry. A few even have jetpacks!

HOW DOES YODA CHANGE THE COURSE OF A BATTLE?

Double cockpits for pilot and co-pilot

Anti-personnel cannon

ON THE SCORCHED and dusty planet of Geonosis, the Jedi have fought bravely, but find themselves outnumbered by Count Dooku's Separatist battle droids. Just when all seems lost, Yoda arrives with a surprise: the Grand Army of the Republic. This force of armored clone troopers turns the tide of the battle and saves the day.

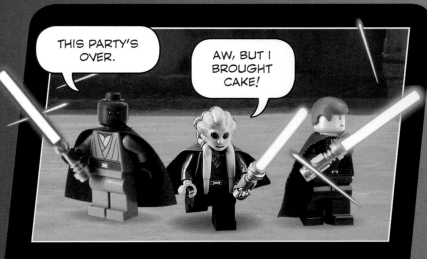

THIS PARTY'S OVER.

AW, BUT I BROUGHT CAKE!

JEDI IN TROUBLE
Force powers and the ability to block laser bolts with a lightsaber make a single Jedi more than a match for most opponents. But up against thousands of battle droids, even Mace Windu and his team need help. Without Yoda, the battle would be lost.

Troop bay

Composite-
beam pinpoint
laser turret

YODA TO THE RESCUE
The Jedi Master takes command of the clone army and directs his Republic gunships to aid the Jedi on Geonosis. Their arrival is a complete surprise to the Separatists, who thought they had beaten the Jedi. Yoda's army reinvigorates the Republic's fight and Count Dooku flees.

The **Republic gunship** is a familiar sight during the Clone Wars. Also known as Low Altitude Assault Transports (LAATs), these **powerful** ships transport dozens of **clone troopers** in their open central sections.

AGAINST THE SEPARATISTS
The Battle of Geonosis marks the beginning of the Clone Wars. Although the Jedi do not lose this battle, they have far from won the war. Under Yoda's expert leadership, the Republic army battles the Separatists all over the galaxy. On world after world, Yoda's wise strategies help the clone troopers and their Jedi generals to score important victories against the ever-expanding ranks of droid legions.

JABBA THE HUTT

THE INFAMOUS JABBA the Hutt is a powerful slug-like crime lord with a palace full of tough alien henchmen. Jabba would love to have some Jedi lightsabers of his own—even if he has to make the sound effects himself!

Stone and durasteel construction

<I WOULD PAY A GREAT BOUNTY FOR A WORKING LIGHTSABER.> *

* TRANSLATED FROM HUTTESE

Jabba's assistant, Bib Fortuna

Hookah pipe

I'D BE HAPPY TO JUST GET A DAY OFF!

Twi'lek dancer Oola

Salacious Crumb, a Kowakian monkey-lizard

Bounty hunter Boushh

Gamorrean guard watchman

JABBA'S PALACE

Jabba's palace lies on the edge of the Northern Dune Sea on Tatooine. It's not easy to sneak inside, but when Yoda's students' lightsabers end up in Jabba's slimy clutches, that's just what the young Padawans have to do!

Yoda once sent **Anakin** Skywalker and his apprentice Ahsoka to rescue Jabba's **kidnapped** son **Rotta**. The act earned the Republic permission to fly its **ships** through Hutt space … and gained Yoda the **respect** of the mighty Jabba.

Gun stash

RANCOR PIT

Beneath a trap door in Jabba's throne room is the lair of the fearsome Rancor. Jabba's favorite sport is dropping unwelcome visitors into this pit, where they must battle for survival against the hulking monster—or else find a very good hiding place, and fast!

Fortified palace entrance

Twi'lek head-tails

Pointed teeth

BIB FORTUNA

Bib Fortuna is a Twi'lek from the planet Ryloth, and is Jabba's assistant, majordomo, and occasional sail barge pilot. Despite his extra-big brain, he is surprisingly easy to fool—both by Force mind tricks and by droid distractions that help Jedi younglings creep past!

DATA FILE

- **HOMEWORLD:** NAL HUTTA
- **BIRTH DATE:** 600 BBY
- **POSITION:** CRIME LORD
- **CLAN:** DESILIJIC
- **WEIGHT:** 1,358 KG (2,994 POUNDS)

41

HOW DOES A GENERAL TRAVEL IN STYLE?

WHETHER MEDITATING in the Jedi Temple or flying through hyperspace, a Jedi Master's life is seldom one of luxury. The Republic frigate that carries General Yoda on his vital missions across the galaxy may look big, but most of the space is taken up by clone troopers and crew.

Rotating turbolaser cannon

Twin laser turret

I CALL DIBS ON DRIVING!

Navigational sensor dish

COCKPIT
The frigate's cockpit is fitted with a weapons-targeting system and an advanced navicomputer for negotiating faster-than-light travel. It is designed for a Republic captain, but it is sometimes piloted by Jedi generals such as Quinlan Vos.

Main forward sensors

Retrofitted *Consular*-class cruiser

CONFERENCE ROOM

When a general is not able to be there in person, a hologram is the second-best choice. The frigate is equipped with a long-distance communications system that can send and receive signals from other star systems. This enables Yoda to speak with his fellow Jedi Council members— or receive urgent messages from Chancellor Palpatine.

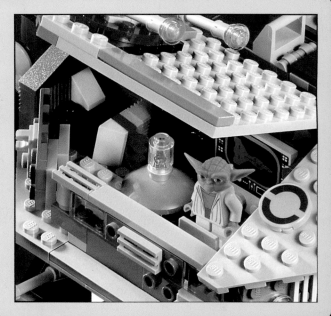

Communication antenna

Long-range sensor dish

Open Circle Fleet symbol

Sublight engine

ESCAPE POD

The escape pod sits under the cockpit. This was originally a salon built for diplomats and other important passengers before the diplomatic vessel was converted to a military warship. In an emergency, this self-contained, armored chamber can be detached from the main vehicle and launched into space.

Yoda was once on board a frigate that was **ambushed** by Separatists. He used one of the ship's **escape pods** to safely reach a nearby **moon**.

YODA'S GALAXY

THE GALAXY IS A BIG PLACE, but you can see quite a lot of it if you live to be almost 900 years old. Yoda has visited many worlds on his interplanetary adventures—some of which he'd like to return to more than others!

NABOO

"A lovely vacation spot this is. From Naboo many well-known beings come: Senator Amidala, Supreme Chancellor Palpatine, and the famous Gungan Jar Jar Binks. Enjoyed I did, going for a refreshing swim to the Gungan city, and the ducks I fed by the Royal Palace. Recommend it I do, but for Sith Lords, watch out you should."

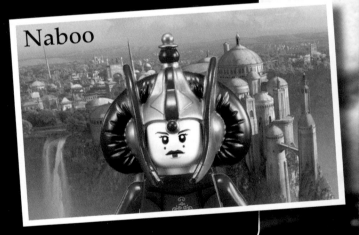

Naboo

GEONOSIS

"Like bugs and battle droids, you do? Then to Geonosis go you should. With a large group of new clone friends here I came, and an old student bumped into I did. Had to leave in a hurry Count Dooku did, heh heh! Heard I have a new Sith Academy setting up Dooku is. Drop in again soon I may."

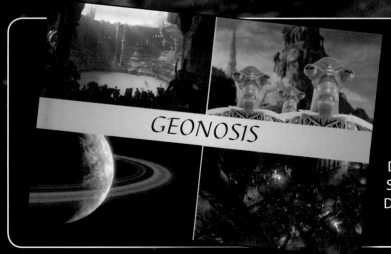

GEONOSIS

CORUSCANT

"Noise. Traffic. Politics. Care for these things I do not. But here is the Jedi Temple, so here too am I! One giant city the planet Coruscant is, capital of the Republic. Important decisions the Jedi Council makes, such as which younglings to train and where to go for lunch. Not easy it is to get 12 Jedi Masters to agree!"

HOTH

"For contemplation and self-discovery a good place the ice world Hoth is. Mostly your own freezing point discover you will. Very scenic the glaciers and caves are, if hungry wampas you avoid. Send the Padawans here on their next field trip, I shall. Meet any dangerous clone warriors, I hope they will not!"

TATOOINE

"To this planet of twin suns I once traveled. Badly sunburnt I got (not well do green and red skin mix!). In Mos Eisley, stolen my luggage was. Smelled like bantha fodder, my hotel room did. Suggest visiting here I do not."

Greetings from Tatooine

45

YODA'S ALLY OR ENEMY?
JEK-14

The **Kyber** crystal has the power to create Force-enhanced **clones**. Long ago it was split up and **hidden** in Padawan lightsabers. But Dooku sends Grievous to **steal** the pieces and reunites them.

Eyes crackle with inner power

Ultra-powerful lightsaber blade

COUNT DOOKU PLANS to use a stolen Kyber crystal to build an entire army of Force-powered Sith clones. The first of his new warriors is the mighty Jek-14—will he prove to be Yoda's friend, or his most dangerous foe?

BUILT FOR DESTRUCTION
Jek's glowing arm has been infused with the energy of the Kyber crystal. He can fire beams of deadly Force lightning, transform his arm into a shield to repel attacks, and perform powerful Force pushes. He is also an excellent pilot and is skilled with a lightsaber. Even just emerged from a cloning tube, he poses a serious threat to Yoda and other Jedi in battle.

Modified clone trooper helmet

Armored bodysuit provides protection in combat

projects Force shields and lightning

DATA FILE

- **HOMEWORLD:** KAMINO
- **BIRTH DATE:** 21 BBY
- **RANK:** SITH CLONE
- **TRAINED BY:** COUNT DOOKU
- **WEAPON:** FORCE-ENHANCED ARM, BLUE-BLADED LIGHTSABER

Astromech droid socket

Elevating laser cannon

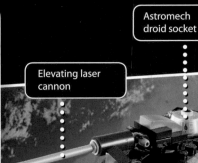

STEALTH STARFIGHTER

Jek-14 conducts his missions aboard his stealth starfighter, a sleek black ship that can slip into systems undetected and escape into hyperspace without a trace. His ability to control matter with his Kyber-powered arm lets him disassemble and reassemble his starfighter at will.

Wings adjust for maneuvers and space battle

Tally marks keep count of victories

Sensor-deflecting hull plating

Powerful engines leave enemies far behind

GALAXY'S MOST WANTED

Count Dooku has given Jek the rage and strength of the dark side of the Force, but Yoda senses the mercy and goodness of the light side in him as well. With both Jedi and Sith pursuing him, Jek must decide which half of his dual nature he will ultimately choose.

AN UNKNOWN DESTINY

In the end, Jek decides that he must find his own path in the galaxy. He departs, warning both Yoda and Count Dooku to leave him alone. Yoda is sad to see him go, but he suspects that if Jek ever returns, it will be as an ally and friend.

YOU KNOW WHAT TO DO.

Clone commander CC-1004, nicknamed "Gree"

Order 66 is a contingency plan for dealing with the **Jedi Order** should the Jedi ever become a **threat** to the Republic. When the clone troopers receive the Order 66 **command**, they betray their Jedi allies with **deadly** consequences.

WHEN WAS YODA'S DARKEST HOUR?

THE GREATEST BETRAYAL that Yoda ever faces comes when Supreme Chancellor Palpatine commands the Clone Army to turn on their Jedi generals. Most of the Jedi fall to the unexpected attack. Just a few scattered survivors remain, on the run from the forces of Emperor Palpatine's newly established Empire.

> THIS JEDI IS IN BIG TROUBLE!

41st Elite Corps clone trooper

Holographic image of Palpatine

CLONE CRISIS

Yoda has relied on his clone troopers on dozens of planets during the Clone Wars, and he trusts them to always carry out their missions. During the Battle of Kashyyyk, Yoda knows that Commander Gree will faithfully follow his orders—he just doesn't realize whose orders the clone commander will follow first!

ORDER 66

As part of his plan to take over the galaxy, Supreme Chancellor Palpatine contacts the clone commanders and executes Order 66—a secret instruction that declares the Jedi to be traitors to the Republic. It is the beginning of a new regime and the fall of the old Jedi Order.

> TRY THAT AGAIN, THEY WILL NOT!

> WELL, MAYBE ONE MORE TIME...

END OF AN ERA

Through the Force, Yoda senses the danger just in time and turns the tables on his would-be assassins. With the help of his Wookiee friends, Yoda flees Kashyyyk aboard a small escape pod. He travels to Coruscant to meet with fellow fugitive Obi-Wan Kenobi and to confront the new Emperor.

YODA VS.

THERE ARE TWO SIDES to the Force. The light side is an ally to Yoda, but the dark side poses great danger. Darth Sidious is the most powerful dark side follower. He and Yoda are matched in strength, but draw on opposing sides of the Force.

THE PATH OF TRUTH AND GOODNESS, THE LIGHT SIDE IS.

THE LIGHT SIDE

Jedi spend their lives studying the light side of the Force. Through focus and meditation, they achieve inner balance and an enhanced awareness of the universe. The Force grants them great power and knowledge, which they use to uphold peace and justice in the galaxy.

- WISDOM

- COMPASSION

- INNER STRENGTH

- LOYALTY

- JUSTICE

THE DARK SIDE

> BUT MY SIDE HAS COOL OUTFITS AND RED LIGHTSABERS!

THE DARK SIDE

For every light, there is a shadow. Those who cross over to the dark side of the Force are fueled by negative emotions such as greed and rage. The dark side offers them almost unlimited power— but this comes at a cost, damaging their bodies and even their minds.

- SECRET TEACHINGS
- PASSION
- TERRIFYING POWER
- JEALOUSY
- DESTRUCTION

THE EMPIRE

YODA GOES INTO HIDING as a dark new order rises to replace the Republic. The Empire rules the galaxy through oppression and fear, tightening its grip to crush all resistance and keep unhappy worlds under control.

Superlaser weapon

EMPEROR PALPATINE

Face and eyes distorted by dark side energies

With his true face revealed at last, the former Chancellor now reigns supreme as the Emperor. Yoda's greatest foe is enormously powerful in the dark side of the Force. His only weakness is his misguided belief that no one can stand against him.

The Emperor has no need for fancy clothing

A second Death Star is built after its predecessor was destroyed by Luke Skywalker and the Rebel Alliance.

DATA FILE

- **HOMEWORLD:** NABOO
- **BIRTH DATE:** 82 BBY
- **RANK:** EMPEROR
- **TRAINED BY:** DARTH PLAGUEIS
- **WEAPON:** FORCE LIGHTNING

For all of his **wisdom** and experience, even Yoda never **guesses** that the Emperor's **defeat** will come at the hands of **Darth Vader**.

STORMTROOPERS

Protected by suits of plastoid armor, the clones who once fought on Yoda's side in the Republic have become the Empire's army of obedient stormtroopers. If any of them are still loyal to their old Jedi generals, they definitely hide it well!

Exposed internal structure

DARTH VADER

As the Emperor's right-hand man, the Sith Lord once known as Anakin Skywalker has sworn to hunt down the last of the Jedi Knights. But soon there is another Jedi —because Yoda has trained Anakin's son, Luke Skywalker, to someday face his father.

Red-bladed Sith lightsaber

Pressurized helmet

Chest control panel

Armor with built-in life support

THE DEATH STAR

The Empire's ultimate weapon, the Death Star is a moon-sized space station that can deconstruct a planet with a single blast. When the first Death Star destroys Alderaan, Yoda can sense the disturbance in the Force all the way on Dagobah.

DATA FILE

HOMEWORLD: TATOOINE

REBIRTH DATE: 19 BBY

RANK: SITH LORD

TRAINED BY: OBI-WAN KENOBI, EMPEROR PALPATINE

WEAPON: RED-BLADED LIGHTSABER

LUKE SKYWALKER

YODA HAS TRAINED many Jedi over the centuries. But few have been as important to the fate of the galaxy—or as challenging to teach—as the adventurous and brave young Luke Skywalker.

Anakin Skywalker's old lightsaber

FROM FARMBOY TO JEDI

The farmboy from Tatooine brings a new hope to the few surviving Jedi and the Rebel Alliance against the Empire. Yoda senses that the Force is strong in Luke, but his impatience and lack of discipline remind Yoda of Luke's long-lost father, Anakin.

DATA FILE

- **HOMEWORLD:** TATOOINE
- **BIRTH DATE:** 19 BBY
- **RANK:** JEDI MASTER
- **TRAINED BY:** OBI-WAN KENOBI AND YODA
- **WEAPON:** BLUE- AND LATER GREEN-BLADED LIGHTSABER

Loose-fitting clothing for a desert planet

MEETING YODA

Instructed by the spirit of Obi-Wan Kenobi, Luke travels to Dagobah in search of a great Jedi warrior to train him. But Luke is surprised to discover that the mysterious "Yoda" he seeks is a strange little green creature whose first lesson is that appearances can be deceiving.

PRINCESS LEIA

When Anakin Skywalker's twins are born, Yoda decides that they should be hidden and raised apart to keep them safe. While Luke is sent to Tatooine, his sister Leia becomes a princess of Alderaan. She is also a secret leader of the Rebel Alliance.

"I'M LOOKING FOR A GREAT WARRIOR."

LUKE TO YODA

CELEBRATED PILOT

Like his father, Luke's strong connection to the Force makes him a naturally skilled starfighter pilot. Thanks to this talent, the young Jedi is able to blow up the Death Star on his first flight in an X-wing fighter, saving the Rebel Alliance from destruction by the Empire!

R2-D2 in astromech socket

Laser cannon

S-foil wings open for combat

I SURE HOPE THE FORCE IS WITH ME RIGHT NOW!

Proton torpedo launcher

HAN SOLO

Roguish smuggler Han Solo was drawn into the fight against the Empire when his battered ship, the *Millennium Falcon*, was chartered by Luke and Obi-Wan. The ship was once a flying nightclub owned by Lindo Calrissian and his son Lando. Long ago, they gave Yoda a much-needed lift to the planet Kamino.

SOLO DUO

Han Solo and Yoda go way back. As a child, Han disguised himself as a Jedi Padawan named Ian, and the unlikely pair of heroes shared an action-packed outer space adventure.

Tree roots wrap around hut

YODA'S HUT

It may not be as luxurious as a Jedi Temple, but this humble hut has everything Yoda requires. Built into the base of a large tree, its walls are a mix of mud and parts from the escape pod that Yoda used to travel to Dagobah.

Entrance—watch your head!

HOME SWEET HOME, THIS IS!

Creeping vines grow everywhere

YODA AT HOME

Sleeping chamber

WELCOME TO DAGOBAH!

When you're the Empire's number one Most Wanted, it's the perfect place to hide out and wait for the galaxy's new hope to arrive. Who needs technology and civilization when you've got weeds, muck, and weird creatures to keep you company?

SECRET COMPARTMENT

Yoda took a few important Jedi relics with him on his flight from Coruscant. Among the most precious is his lightsaber. Yoda keeps his weapon safely hidden in a secret space underneath his small but cozy bed.

YODA'S KITCHEN

Inside his hut's small cooking area, Yoda stirs up a variety of nutritious stews and other meals made from local plants and wildlife. His culinary concoctions may not sound (or look or smell) tasty to most humanoids, but to Yoda, they're delicious!

Walking stick can be used as a stirring rod

You'd rather not know …

MMMM. GOOD … AND VERY TASTY.

RECIPE FOR "SWAMP SURPRISE"

* Fresh cloud-tree root
* 3 bog slugs (orange, not blue!)
* 5 spoonfuls of swamp sludge
* A pinch of powdered nightbat toenail
* 8 pebbles (any size)
* 3-4 gimer stick shavings
* Marshworm spice to taste

Dump ingredients into a small pot. Bring to a boil. Gently stir (not too much or the slug flavor will be diluted). Simmer for three weeks. Serve with toadstools and enjoy!

SURPRISINGLY SPACIOUS ON THE INSIDE IT IS, HMM?

Cooking fire

Bottle of mysterious liquid

Barrel collects rainwater for drinking

Walls reinforced with salvaged escape pod pieces

YES, IF YOU'RE IN TUNE with the Force! With the right mindset and training, a person can use this energy to accomplish incredible feats, from sensing the future to taming wild beasts. Luke Skywalker learns much about the Force from Yoda. He is surprised to discover that someone as small as the old Jedi Master can lift something as huge as an X-wing starfighter—just by raising his hand!

SURE, I CAN LIFT IT. I JUST NEED TO BUILD A REALLY BIG CRANE ...

Luke Skywalker

Closed S-foils

Who knows what hungry creatures lurk beneath the swamp's surface?

Landing gear is useless in sticky swamp muck.

X-WING? (WITHOUT TOUCHING IT?)

I COULD TOTALLY DO IT, BUT NOBODY EVER ASKS!

R2-D2

JUDGE ME BY MY SIZE, DO YOU? HAH! SEE WHAT I CAN DO!

CRASH COURSE

On Dagobah, Yoda has only a short time to teach Luke to become a Jedi Knight in order to save the galaxy from the Emperor's evil plans. Yoda does his best to help Luke to understand how to feel the Force, how to ignore distractions, and … how to move rocks while balancing upside down with his teacher standing on his foot! Nobody said Jedi training is easy.

Clinging Dagobah marsh weeds

What else can the **Force** do? Someone who is skilled in it can **jump** amazing distances, block blaster **shots** with a lightsaber, and **influence** the thoughts of small-minded bad guys!

WHAT IS YODA'S LEGACY?

AFTER 900 YEARS, age finally catches up with Yoda. But even after he becomes one with the Force, Yoda and his teachings continue to affect the fate of the galaxy. Yoda's final student, Luke Skywalker, succeeds in defeating the power of the Empire, bringing an end to the Emperor's tyrannical rule and at last restoring balance to the Force.

THE FINAL BATTLE
On the second Death Star, Luke faces Darth Vader in a titanic lightsaber duel. With the wisdom he has gained from Yoda, Luke reaches out to his father, who has long been buried beneath Vader's mask and armor. Freed from the dark side, Anakin Skywalker destroys Emperor Palpatine, and with him the might of the Sith.

Darth Vader must choose between his allegiance to the Emperor and his son

JOIN ME, MY SON.

NO. YOU JOIN ME, FATHER!

New lightsaber constructed by Luke

Mechanical hand

Circular viewport into space

LOOK, SOMEONE JOIN SOMEBODY ALREADY!

A **Jedi's** passing is not necessarily the **end**. Although his physical form disappears, Yoda **continues** to watch over Luke as a **Force spirit**.

Emperor's throne

GONE BUT NEVER FORGOTTEN

Luke goes on to become a great Jedi Master. He builds a new Jedi Order for the reborn New Republic, always guided and inspired by the lessons of his wise old teacher. Through the Holocron recordings stored in the Jedi Library on Coruscant, young Jedi will continue to learn from Yoda's knowledge and experience for many generations to come.

Imperial throne room at the top of a 100-story tower

GLOSSARY

BATTLE DROID
A Separatist robot designed for combat.

BOUNTY HUNTER
Someone who is hired to track down or destroy people or objects for money.

CHANCELLOR
The title given to the head of the Republic.

CHOSEN ONE
A person spoken of in an old Jedi prophecy who will bring balance to the Force.

CLONE TROOPERS
Soldiers of the Republic Clone Army. They are identical because they share the same genes.

CLONE WARS
A series of galaxy-wide battles fought between the Republic's Clone Army and the Separatist Droid Army, which took place between 22 and 19 BBY.

CYBORG
A being that is partly a living organism and partly a robot.

DARK SIDE
The evil side of the Force that feeds off negative emotions.

DEATH STAR
An enormous Imperial battle station, which has enough firepower to destroy an entire planet.

DROID
A robot. Droids come in many shapes and sizes and serve a variety of duties.

EMPIRE
A tyrannical power that rules the galaxy under the leadership of Emperor Palpatine, a Sith Lord.

EMPEROR
Ruler of the Empire.

FORCE
The energy that flows through all living things. It can be used for good or evil.

FORCE-ENHANCED CLONE
A Force-powered clone created by Separatist leader and Sith apprentice Count Dooku.

FORCE LEAP
A huge jump made by someone using the Force to enhance their natural ability.

FORCE LIGHTNING
Deadly rays of blue energy used as a weapon.

FORCE PUSH
A blast of energy that a Force-user can use to knock over an opponent.

HOLOCRON
An ancient device that contains large amounts of data. It is activated through use of the Force.

JEDI
A member of the Jedi Order who studies the light side of the Force.

JEDI COUNCIL
Twelve senior Jedi who meet to make important decisions.

JEDI KNIGHT
A full member of the Jedi Order who has completed all of their training.

JEDI GRAND MASTER
The head of the Jedi Order and the greatest and wisest of the Jedi Masters.

JEDI MASTER
An experienced and high-ranking Jedi who has demonstrated great skill and dedication.

KYBER CRYSTAL
A very powerful crystal used in lightsabers. It greatly magnifies the powers of those who are sensitive to the Force.

LIGHTSABER
A sword-like weapon with a blade of pure energy that is used by Jedi and Sith.

LIGHT SIDE
The good side of the Force that brings peace and justice.

LIVING FORCE
The view that the Force is present in all living things. Those who live by this view rely on their instincts and live in the moment.

PADAWAN
A young Jedi apprentice who is in training to become a full-fledged Jedi Knight.

REBEL ALLIANCE
The organization that resists and fights the Empire.

REPUBLIC
The democratic government that rules many planets in the galaxy.

SENATE
The government of the Republic. It is made up of senators from all over the galaxy.

SENATOR
A person who acts as a representative for their planet in the Senate.

SEPARATISTS
An alliance of those who are opposed to the Republic.

SITH
An ancient sect of Force-sensitives who seek to use the dark side of the Force to gain power.

YOUNGLING
A Force-sensitive child who joins the Jedi Order to be trained in the Jedi arts.

DK

LONDON, NEW YORK, MELBOURNE,
MUNICH, AND DELHI

Senior Editors Elizabeth Dowsett
and Helen Murray

Designer Jon Hall

Senior Designer Lisa Sodeau

Pre-Production Producer Rebecca
Fallowfield

Senior Producer Lloyd Robertson

Publishing Manager Julie Ferris

Design Manager Nathan Martin

Art Director Ron Stobbart

Publishing Director Simon Beecroft

Additional photography by Gary Ombler

Dorling Kindersley would like to thank: Randi Sørensen and Louise
Weiss Borup at the LEGO Group; J. W. Rinzler, Chris Gollaher, Leland
Chee, Troy Alders, and Carol Roeder at Lucasfilm; Lisa Stock for
editorial assistance and John Goldsmid for design assistance.

First published in the United States in 2013 by
DK Publishing
375 Hudson Street, New York, New York, 10014

10 9 8 7 6 5 4 3 2 1
001—187438—Aug/13

Published in Great Britain by Dorling Kindersley Limited.

A catalog record for this book is available
from the Library of Congress.

ISBN: 978-1-46540-868-6

Color reproduction by Alta Image, UK
Printed and bound in China by Leo Paper Group

Discover more at
www.dk.com
www.LEGO.com/starwars